That is the lesson for me, for us, for you. You are choosing. Each moment, each word that comes out of your mouth, you are choosing. Each action, you are choosing. Each thought, you are choosing.

When you begin to see that it's futile to blame and say that it's because of someone else, you are beginning to move toward the life you truly want. We can all point to why we "had to" or why they "made us," but truly we choose our thoughts, our reactions, and our life, moment by moment. Take any story of triumph over adversity and you will hear the same thing—I wasn't going to let it stop me. Circumstance is only one factor in life. What we do with ourselves in each moment is all about choice.

DEAR GOD, WHY?

A Spiritual Journey

JILL FAIRWEATHER

Fairweather Center Publishing

DEAR GOD, WHY?
Jill Fairweather

Printed in the United States of America
First Printing, 2015

ISBN-13: 978-0-692-56715-9 (trade paperback)
ISBN-10: 0692567151 (trade paperback)

Published by Fairweather Center Publishing, Abington, MA

Inquiries should be addressed to
The Fairweather Center
HigherRealm@comcast.net
http://www.fairweathercenter.com

Cover Design and Image © Jill Fairweather

Introduction

This is not my life story, but my growth story. There are so many events that were influential to me that I don't write about here. However they are here in the form of the phases of my consciousness wherein they happened.

I realize I am so blessed. I have enjoyed so much abundance in my life. I have had clean water, shelter, and warmth almost every day of my life. Some of us—yes, "us," humans on this planet—are fighting for their lives, have experienced untold loss, trauma, and pain far beyond the challenges I have written about in this book. Yet my hope is that I can inspire someone who reads this, to shift, release some struggles and achieve their own breakthroughs through reading about mine.

This is a story from my point of view. I speak my truth as it is to me now, at this time, although we are ever-evolving. The time has come for me to share my story. We are all unique, and my hope is to inspire you to be more you. Take it or leave it, this is my story for you to help ponder your own past, present and future. I am releasing it in powerful vulnerability with love and compassion for myself and others. We all have issues, however it is hardest to truly see and change our own, so many times we point to others instead. We just all need to love each other the way we are. While choosing what's best for ourselves.

Acknowledgements

Thank you, Michelle, for being the first person I trusted to read the first chapter, Mat for encouraging me, and Maureen and Teresa for editing and improving. Thank you, Leila, for the inspiration and accountability to write this book. Nancy, for the reading that re-awakened my true spirit. Rita, Rhys, Lisa, Carole Lynne, Barbara, and all the other seers and teachers, for the knowledge, insight, and all the messages that have helped me on my path. For my loved ones, thanks for being you. And to Michael, my greatest teacher, thank you. Namaste.

Preface
Where is the Love?

Once upon a time, I had my heart broken. Okay, actually, many times. But this book speaks of the particular journey through a heartbreak that showed me I had been living in denial, reaction, and the dark side of codependence. My husband had an affair, and I thought it was the greatest sin anyone had ever committed. I since realized I was no angel either. Then I found out that blame, such a near and dear friend to me, was a close companion who had never given me much in return. I decided to let go of my friend blame. And it's not been the simplest thing to do.

The things that have hurt me the most are the things that have helped me the most too. Each day of this life is an incredible journey, a sacred gift.

I have learned what forgiveness means to me, and what it doesn't. I offer true forgiveness when I give it, and that consists of loving myself, seeing that others are only showing me how I believe I deserve and want to be treated.

Give 'em an inch, they'll take a mile. To me this doesn't mean that every day, all the time, you have to worry about getting short-changed. However it does mean when the time comes when your loved one or someone closely involved in your life is making a big decision that affects you negatively in ways you cannot accept at the moment, make your demand. Be true to yourself. It's always for the higher good. There's compromise, but when you know that you will be devastated, that it is just not acceptable, you must speak up. Your insides are screaming at you. You can feel it in your body. Listen to yourself! I have realized as I have come to practice this, that I used to be much more hard-lined and hard-edged. I have softened so much by learning to practice loving myself instead of fighting for myself. I have me. All is well.

It seems to me that life comes in waves. Our three-dimensional reality offers time and space for dates, times, and deadlines. But I believe our belief in time also limits us to thinking about "how long" something takes. What the measurement should be to grow up, get married, have children, have pets, buy a house, be successful, retire, travel, etc. Many people work so hard and give up so much of their time for money, and it seems people who follow this need for money the most are those who feel they do not have "enough" or do not feel they are "enough." It is as if these timelines and milestones cause us to measure ourselves, and our success as a person, by something completely outside of our own true desires. Perhaps we are ignoring our passions and our opportunity for more joy.

You *must* make your life about your own happiness and joy. Anyone who does not treat you with kindness and respect shouldn't take a lot of your time, unless you are in a situation where you are receiving pleasure and happiness by giving what you're giving. Life is positive when those closest to you support you, consider you, increase your happiness and lift you higher, and you them.

I do believe in something currently labeled the *Law of Attraction*. It is when you hear someone say "Once I get it in my head…" The Law of Attraction is the determination, the force of will, the thing that Napoleon Hill's book *Think and Grow Rich* describes. It is knowing that our human brain, filterer of our consciousness and our choices, has the power to shape our reality.

Why is it that we show more courtesy and respect to strangers sometimes than we do to our loved ones at home? For example, someone has an annoying trait or habit that you excuse over and over because you don't feel telling them it annoys you will change them, and you don't want to hurt them. It would be silly and mean to tell them that they should change every time they exhibited it. And yet, that's just what we do to those we love the very most.

"But they, but they, but they!" we say. Take a step back. There is no difference. The only difference is that we must live closer to, be more surrounded by, the distasteful aspects of those closest to us. Insisting and reminding does not change anyone. You have choices. There is acceptance, or when acceptance does not seem possible, you can make changes to support your own needs. Discussion could be important in understanding and trying to find compromise; however, you could also just know that looking at life from their side, they and us and everyone else just wants to be loved the way they are, and everyone has their reasons for what they say or do. Having the same discussion over and over about what you don't like is just an unhealthy relationship with life, period.

If someone says they want to change, and asks for help from someone else who can help them, and that person enjoys helping them, then a joint project is created. When one accepts help or guidance they can use from others who willingly give it, and benefit from that help, there is a positive energy exchange. However, if someone wants and tries to make someone else change, and they simply resist, fight back, and become hurt, eventually the repetition of pointing out another person's alleged problem will only force you apart. Sometimes, if someone does something that annoys you, and you try to put yourself in their shoes, you can suddenly see it from another perspective. Maybe it's because that was love in their family, or they want it to be love now. For example, think about how differently each person might want to spend, acknowledge or not acknowledge their own birthday or holidays and how that may be just right for them. Sometimes when this happens, you can just love them more, and your own annoyance at your difference disappears. You suddenly respect your differences and you are not disturbed by them anymore. Needs change along the way. If something becomes the most important thing to you for your well-being and the well-being of those around you, you must make the appropriate changes in *your* life. You have the power of choice.

Are we not recycled, just like fall leads to winter, and winter leads to spring? The leaves on the trees come, and go, and come again. Are we not just cells of the universe called humans? Yes, we have lives, personalities, goals. But what if our lives are just repetitive things, such as becoming a leaf again and again? You think you are different from nature? How on Earth do we make babies, that is, create ourselves? Our very selves. We create each other as humans. Or do we? You don't know how to make a baby, do you? Oh, that's right, you know how babies are made. ☺

Along my way through the last few years, as I describe in this book, I discovered things about me that are truly me, and I began to embrace my unique self. I realized that within every strong fear is the answer to that fear. We are only hiding our gifts from ourselves behind the fear. But when we live in the shadow side of our gifts, we are not seeing them, only the back side of them, which seems to cause us pain and trouble. If we broke through the fear and accepted them, we would come out of the shadows. What do you love? What are you good at? What lights you up? I've discovered that my highest order in this life is making the space for and giving myself acceptance of my gifts. I feel deeply for all makers of art, as I feel they are putting their most intimate selves right out there, whatever their medium, for all to see. And we are blessed by them.

Within these pages I hope that you find transformation. That you see in yourself, for the first time, something that sets you free.

Chapter One
How I Knew I Was Different

When I was four, I was just coming into my physical power. I went to Kathy Corrigan's School of Gymnastics and I could do "no-handed flips." I tried to ride my bike so fast that I crashed into our neighbor's fence and had to get stitches in my chin. I was racing with my best friend. My father was a policeman and rushed me to the hospital in the police car. It was fun, they said I didn't even cry. I also got scarlet fever that Christmas, and thus began many years of physical mishaps, accidents, sicknesses, and hospital visits. I remember hearing way too many times, "Oh, Jilly."

I had many outlets for my energy during elementary school, with gymnastics and other sports. I still had lots of energy at home too, and my family gave me everything they could think of to keep me occupied and out of trouble. I did a lot of reading. I made art, played games, and put together puzzles. I played music on our record player. I played outside a lot too, had a bike and many other toys. I wanted a unicycle, and my parents got me one. I insisted on bringing home a chicken from the class hatching project. One time I even refinished an antique milk can for my mom. I especially loved mystery books, my magic trick set, my swingset, and the fresh pears from the tree in the back yard.

I had a recurring dream that I was this local superhero. I would float up above the trees and down my street. People would point and shout "The Jill!" I also dreamed of war, though. I was a soldier in the war. I was stuck in a dugout and wanted to run away from the war, AWOL. I would wake up from that dream and wonder why I was such a coward. I loved faraway places, secrets and anything foreign to me, and I wanted to believe everything I heard. Everything seemed possible to me, and it didn't seem to matter what was true or untrue.

I had a weird relationship with my teachers at school. I got more attention than the other kids, but looking back, the truth was I demanded it. Just like some of today's children, I was over-stimulated or over-expressive, not sure which, but my teachers and I both knew that I was not as attentive, still, and quiet as they might have liked. I remember my fifth grade teacher saying,

"Jill, let someone else answer," because I always had my hand up. This trend kept on until one day in adulthood, I suddenly realized that because I saw the teachers as authorities, I felt I had to interact with them about every question I had, in order to have the right answer to it. I had not realized that I could be my own authority. I had been terribly confused and disturbed about all the mysterious thoughts, feelings, and places that it seemed were always floating around in my mind.

My grammie seemed to understand me. She would just give me a smile or hold my hand, and made everything okay, even though at the time I thought I was a freak. Grammie would always help me out by eating my vegetables for me too. I hated vegetables.

I swam so much at my uncle's pool that I would be completely waterlogged by the time they dragged me out. There was something special about it. I used to swim back and forth across the pool underwater. There was this beautiful deep silence, accompanied by this tinkling sound from the heavens. I loved it so much. I figured out many years later that it was my silver charms necklace that made the tinkling sound. I felt a little let down, because at the time, it was much more magical than that.

Another thing that seemed curious was that there was a "Mr. Owl" in the tree in our back yard. My sisters and I, along with the three kids from the family down the street, would all stand at the tree and talk to him. There was a Mr. Owl on TV in the Tootsie Roll commercial at the time, but it wasn't *that* Mr. Owl. It seemed to have something to do with me.

I also remember feeling everything so deeply, too deeply. When my sisters had terrible ear infections, and were crying and sick and in pain, my mother was going out of her mind. I felt it too. Beyond having my own ear infection, I felt my sisters' pain, my mom's pain, my dad's pain. I didn't know it then, but I do now. I was picking up everything. I thought it was mine. I wanted it to stop. I didn't know how to make it stop. I began to feel powerless. I began to have fear. I began to have worry. The most upsetting part was that I knew it shouldn't be that way, but I didn't know how to fix it. I felt like I was not fulfilling my superhero status, and I was a total failure.

I felt a little crazy. My friends loved me but pointed it out. I got along best with those who were silly and questioned everything. I loved dressing up, but I was also a tomboy. I liked coming up with new ideas, planning things, and getting excited for them. Sometimes my big plans didn't work out, and I was devastated. Most of the time, though, everything was an adventure, I was looking for the spark in everything. It's quite amazing when I think and feel back to my life as a child. It was pretty intense. I jumped and screamed and grabbed and fell and laughed and talked and wondered and asked and saw a lot. When I was hurt or sick, I was sure that I had brought it on myself by being too much and too fast, that I was different, and that I was a little out of control.

Chapter Two
Why I Didn't Understand Much

There is a distinct line drawn across my early life. I was nine years old when my parents separated. Two years later, we moved from Massachusetts to Washington State. I remember thinking how great it would be to start over where no one knew me. I thought my life would be completely new and different. There was a mental fog. I felt a need to figure things out, to try to get free from the confusion, to be loved, to seek the truth, and know my correct path. I remember sitting by myself wondering how to live life, wondering how would I get through the next day. I remember one day as I was walking with my younger sister home from school in our new home town in Washington, I saw children playing made-up games in their yard, and I noticed how blissful they seemed, without a care in the world. I was jealous. I remember running away from home once after talking back to and arguing with my mom a few years later. I walked uptown in a severe state of frustration. By the time I got there, my purpose was to throw myself in front of the train. Luckily the train didn't come along just then.

Often, in the afternoons, I would ride my unicycle down the street, until I started getting into my teen years, and people started beeping, yelling, and waving at me. I felt embarrassed about the attention, so I switched to my bike instead. I am grateful to my sisters for playing tennis and badminton with me. I was also blessed that my closest friends had vehicles and we could drive around. I started smoking cigarettes because friends told me it was fun, and I thought, "Hey, it's something to do."

I wanted to do more with my body, play more sports and games, but I had trouble with the track team, the volleyball team, and then the softball team. I felt so different, so out of place in the world. I tried very hard to make a place for myself, and I wanted to be popular at school. I was on the student body association, I did volunteer work, and I was a cheerleader. I had always made good grades in school. The only thing the teachers would complain about was my inability to remain attentive and focused. Even though I was proud of my achievements, none of them seemed to feel right. I was looking outside myself for someone to validate me and tell me I was okay. I did well with gymnastics into my high school years, and had a job as the assistant teacher/coach. This light in my life was thanks to my boss and coach. I loved her, and her daughter was on the team too. Sometimes I was invited to their home since we lived nearby. She would give me a ride when we went to other gyms. I remember admiring her family. I wondered how they stayed together when my parents had not. I looked for clues.

It seemed like many adults had something to say to me, a message to impart. Perhaps it was my questioning nature, or maybe the world was just like that, but I took in everything they said. They would say things like "Don't do" this, or "Make sure you do" that, or "You should be proud to be tall," or "Don't let anyone tell you..." Blah blah blah. I kept trying to reconcile it all. There were also the nasty things that other students would say. I was very skinny and didn't start developing or get my first period until I was sixteen. I didn't have a boyfriend, except for one very brief, innocent romance over the summer. My sisters and I traveled back to Massachusetts to spend the whole summer with our dad and stepmom. We had a lot of fun during the summer, and some fabulous family vacations that money couldn't buy. They were so good at finding ways to do fun things for not a lot of money. My mom always made things special too. I am glad my parents parted when the relationship wasn't working. Another reason life felt strange though, not only having the other parent(s) out of daily life for an extended time, but that time with one parent was a vacation, time with the other was school and a single mom who worked full time.

I always felt as though I was the black sheep, the failure. I was embarrassed because it seemed I drew attention to myself for making mistakes. Looking back now, I see clearly that I was full of untapped energy and attention deficit. I felt restricted in many ways because I couldn't fulfill myself and get all the things I wanted, and I had so much extra physical and mental energy. I was like a caged animal. I had awesome friends and lots of great activities. Still, I felt so unfulfilled. I wanted more.

I was also very interested in romance and sex. My parents talked to us about sex, but it just made me feel as though I was missing the natural ways of life and love and didn't know what they were supposed to be or how to find them. I felt that I needed to figure things out or I would remain unfulfilled in romance too. I had romantic encounters with two different boys separately at the end of high school. Or at least *I* had romantic feelings and expectations. They both were after sex. I knew and liked both boys very much, but they each took advantage of me. I didn't really even know what was happening except that it was exciting to be wanted and scary to be doing adult things I had no experience with. I clearly said "No" when it was going too far, but unfortunately I lost my virginity this way, in the dark, on the floor, in a few short moments when that boy did not take no for an answer. I never saw or spoke to him again. I wasn't even sure what happened and it took a few days to sort it out. I didn't realize that it wasn't my fault, only that I had made another mistake, a huge one. I had not intended to have sex and give up my precious virginity until it felt right. It was only twenty-three years later that I realized what had really happened, and how it had affected me.

There was so much that was good in my life, but I couldn't see it except when I was buried in it. So I was always looking for something to bury myself in. This need to always bury myself in something lasted until my late thirties. I was on a quest to "be" that was born of what felt like outside forces pushing me hard, beyond anything I could even understand. I always thought that whatever new thing I was going for would solve every-thing, like it was the missing piece. It never was.

Chapter Three
Becoming Fun Again

When I had just graduated from high school, I made my last summer visit to Massachusetts. I decided to stay and live with my dad and stepmom at the end of the summer. My mom, being very strict, had done a great job of protecting me. She protected the four of us, actually, as a single mom. Our house, car, our money—somehow she made it work. I am so grateful now. But at the time, I felt trapped, geeky, weird, and unpopular. Now I was back East with just myself, my dad, and my stepmom in our household. I had a job, I finally got my driver's license and a checking account, and I felt a sense of independence and control. I am so grateful to my dad and stepmom.

I remember the first time I drove by myself. I was sent to the store for a few groceries because a hurricane was coming. What a great thing! I was gifted with my great-aunt's car, and I loved it. I had a radio installed, and I was on top of the world, driving in my own car with my radio on.

I started college at night in September. All new experiences, and new people. I loved my job as a secretary, which my stepmom helped me get at the same company where she worked. I made a regular paycheck and I had a fabulous time using computerized software to manage my money at home. We went shopping at lunchtime for work clothes. I had never had so many clothes and shoes that I chose myself in my life! I felt so grown up. I was also going to church with my parents and joined the choir, the hand bell choir, and the youth group as a leader. I helped out with the church fair and took up skiing too.

I was also looking for romance. I didn't realize that I was subconsciously desperate to undo my first experiences by replacing them with better ones. I did not have the tools or self-respect to know what I deserved or how to get it. I was looking for any cute guy to pay attention to me. I was still picky about guys, and said no to most of them. I certainly liked their attention, though. I made a few friends at school and would hang out with them. They were sexually active, and I got quite an earful. I went to as many parties as I could. It was all so new and exciting.

Soon enough, I wanted to move on campus and attend school full-time. Classes were interesting, but I really was not focused on my education. It was the social scene that I craved. I wanted to be in the party dorm. I hadn't really wanted to attend college right away. I had intended to go to school back in Washington with my classmate and close friend. I was attracted to the idea of getting an apartment together and attending the same school. When it didn't happen, I decided to stay in Massachusetts. My dad offered to pay for school. I didn't really have the clarity or mental space to think things over or to speak my mind. I just did what I was offered, since it seemed easier than my own uncertain plan. I was grateful to have more freedom than I could ever remember having. One belief I have, which I hear repeated all the time, is that everything happens for a reason. The way I believe that means that regrets don't matter, regrets are just baggage and guilt, since you can't change the past. I missed my family and friends back home, but I was having too much fun to let it get to me. I very much enjoyed my classes and teachers: media arts, interpersonal communication, photography, philosophy, psychology, and more.

One incredible fear and anxiety in my memory, and something I overcame in this period of my life, was meeting people. When I first moved on campus, I really didn't know anyone. The college friends I had to that point were commuters like me. I would go to the cafeteria for lunch and dinner. As I entered, they swiped my meal card, I would go to the line for food, and I would begin discreetly but desperately looking around for where I could sit. It seemed most people already had friends they were there with. I felt I had a very short one-to-two minute time frame to make this decision, or else I would be humiliated, conspicuously wandering around obviously without a friend in the world. At five foot eleven, somehow I didn't realize I was already conspicuous. This is how I ended up meeting my awesome core group of friends that stayed together for the next couple of years; I asked if I could sit with them. We had a lot of fun together. We did lots of things both on and off campus. I felt that I belonged. This was a talented and caring group of people. Although we were just kids, we formed bonds and share memories of some of the "best of times." Of course there was music, intoxication, and more. Sometimes there was drama. But it all fed my soul and my quest for connection with others and living the bigger life I had been searching for. I hardly remember the drama now, although it tore me apart at the time. One thing that is abundantly clear to me now is that during that period of my life, I became fun again. I recaptured the true spirit of me, the searching, game-for-almost-anything, wide-eyed childlike fearlessness that felt like the real me. My grades were not what I was capable of, and soon it all came to an end when my dad gave me the tough love that a good parent would: an ultimatum that if things did not improve I would not be going to school anymore. They did not, so school came to an early end and within a year I had also moved out. That is how this chapter of my life came to an end.

Chapter Four
Defenses and Revenge

This chapter was hard to write. It's about the ways I sabotaged myself while trying to avoid being hurt. I realize now I was trying to avoid intimacy. Working to manipulate the outcome instead of just stating my needs and wants. Trying to avoid being vulnerable. I felt that my heart was broken many times by many different people. I see so clearly now that was just what I was asking for. I was assuming they would, and operating in a defensive state instead of being open and trusting in myself. Fear and anger were my strongest emotions, with passion mixed in. Woven through the mess, of course, was my true self, the one who jumps in with both feet and wants to make the deepest of connections with others, especially those to whom I feel close. I would go deeply into the relationship with my passionate heart and boundless energy, but I'd also bring my faulty discernment and lack of boundaries along with me. There are dramas upon dramas I could write about. The truth is, I am not "cured" of this yet, either, and it would be smug to think I am. I believe it is all part of the human condition, the ego mind itself, that tries to separate ourselves from, compare ourselves to, and fear our interactions with others sometimes. As long as I have this human mind, it is an ongoing, fulfilling and humbling practice to transcend its limiting or self-depraving thoughts.

In many situations, I would subconsciously and even consciously consider myself a victim. "They" took my deepest secrets and used them against me. They threatened to kill me because they were so angry. They told me I ruined their life. They fired me because I wouldn't have sex with them. They said if I didn't do what they wanted, they would die. They told me I was crazy. They said I was the most self-centered person they ever met. They said I hurt them to the core. They told me I had done a horrible thing and I should know what it is, even though I didn't. They blew me off at the last minute time after time. They would say things about me behind my back, and insult me to my face. They took my dignity by telling me who I was and who I was not, what I was to do, as if I had no choice. They reneged on our agreements. They told me they wished they'd never met me. They said I was arrogant. They said I thought I was better than them.

When I was a young adult and first on my own after leaving school and my dad's, there were traumas with love, money, broken-down cars, moving, emergency health issues, changing of jobs. Somehow I always survived, even though as I went through trauma and drama, I didn't know how I would, especially emotionally. I literally fell apart and put myself back together time after time. I always had a job, and I always felt productive at work, where my goals were clear and I could aim my abundant energy. Before I learned what I learned that brought me to writing this book, life was much more lived in this defenses and revenge mode. And yet, I am grateful for the strength I gained by enduring and becoming wiser for it all. I also feel that my health issues were my anger turned inward, and a subconscious repression of my emotional and physical energy.

The greatest "defenses and revenge," though, were my romantic relationships. My first real love, the first one I *chose* to be sexually involved with, broke my heart over and over. He did not love me the way I loved him. Yet it felt so good, the depth of the feelings, and my love for him. He was such a sweet and honest person. I hung on for dear life. After he broke it off, I remember resolving not to put myself in that position again. I purposely decided that I would not commit to anyone, thereby attempting to avoid the same pain. I remember proudly telling my next boyfriend, who, by the way, was "quite a catch," as they say, that I was still "seeing my ex." I made this new boyfriend quite mad a couple of times with my reckless attitude. There were no cell phones or email back then, so when you kept someone waiting, it was very rude. I was only superficially exploring the relationship, ignoring my deeper feelings for him and my longing to create a deep and mutual commitment. He wasn't going to play along indefinitely. He moved on. I still don't know if his feelings had deepened or if he just wasn't willing to put up with my attitude. I was upset because I thought I could have my cake and eat it too, and I felt like a fool. I breezed right by the possibilities in that relationship, with my defenses and revenge driving the bus.

I spent my mid-twenties in a relationship with a young man I wanted to marry. Although in my mind there were many things to be worked out if we could make it as a married couple, I never tried too hard to work them out. I would bring them up, and the short answers I received, I took as the final answer and just moved on, with yet another chink in my armor. I assumed that my side of things was just not going to be heard and I had to stuff my concerns. Only on certain small things that made me absolutely nuts would I fight back. And it seemed I always had to fight. I couldn't just talk. After four years together, my resentment became all I could see. For the next year,

I attempted to break up with him, but I kept thinking he knew better than me when he said we belonged together. In truth, I slowly broke us down. At the time, I felt I was proving to him that we didn't belong together so he would let me go. That is another form of manipulation I practiced back then, all the while thinking that I was protecting myself. I thought I had to make someone else see my view without just clearly stating and believing it myself. By the time it was really over, after five years together, I completely blamed him for everything. I felt he had controlled me, put me down, and criticized me. I also felt he had slowly removed me from all my friends and my outside interests. I put up a wall between us, and pushed him away forever. It took all my strength, because I loved him. I was very angry. He was a monster to me. Now, I know that I did not do my part to know and speak my truth, calmly and authentically, and that a relationship going bad is not only one person's fault. I apologize that it took me another ten years to realize this and own my part in the problem. I wrote a lot of poems, journals, and letters in that phase of my life. When I got them back out and read them years later, it helped me to see my past in a different way. My former self was a different person. She was a victim.

My most powerfully transformational relationship was with the man I married. I write about this in the next chapters. What we went through with each other over many years together was, well, to use the word of the day, epic. What I see now is that when we met, I took all of the pain and anger from my past, decided it was banished forever, and that this love of my life was someone I could trust and someone I would be happy with for the rest of my life. I was prepared for discussing my truths, and working out any issues. Yet, when we had trouble communicating, I always blamed him for being the one who did not have proper relationship skills. I saw myself as the one who was ready, willing, and able to partner and compromise and prosper together. I had decided that we belonged together. I could see deep into his soul, and I admired him for so many reasons. I could see who he was, that he wanted what I wanted, even if he could not fully express it. This blame game went on until I discovered that no matter what choices I made in support of the relationship that ended up hurting me, I could not blame him for those choices. If the relationship wasn't working, I could change it, change myself, find a way to talk about it without blaming, or otherwise leave it if there were no options left. It was not loving or authentic to stay in it, demanding that the other person change and that we fulfill our potential as a loving couple, on my schedule, just because I wanted that and thought it was possible. This was codependence. Having a purpose of "working it out," while all the time seeing the other person as the one at fault, is not working it out at all. It does not matter who says or does what, it is your own attitude that is running the show. What was missing was me focusing on *my own* expression of *my own* full potential, regardless of who is on that journey with me. I had to let go of my love, several times. I had to let go of my desire for him to change and for us to work out. They are lessons for which I am grateful. I desire for myself and all humans to be free from our mind's need to control and manipulate outcomes. I do not need to classify myself or anyone as right or wrong. I am not my past. I am my present.

∽

And love is never love, that cannot give love up.
—T. McGrath

Should you want to contain something, you must deliberately let it expand. Should you want to take something away, you must deliberately grant it access. Should you want to eliminate something, you must deliberately allow it to flourish.

—Tao

To be aware of a single shortcoming in oneself is more useful than to be aware of a thousand in someone else.
—The Dalai Lama

Chapter Five
Becoming a Workaholic

I was always saying "I'm bored" as a kid. It must have been tough being my parent or teacher. There's a special place in my heart for kids like this. I know it's an abundance of energy that, if properly channeled, would be positive. However, a child doesn't always have the knowledge, power, or resources to follow their energy, their knowing, their heart's desires. Today, many are given medication to help them behave and fit in. In my own life, I came to be a workaholic. Working seemed to use up all my energy, which solved some problems at the time. It was an easy thing to become, especially self-employed in a boom time of real estate. I had been a waitress for four years in my mid-twenties; although I worked six to seven days a week with a couple of doubles a week at the time, I wasn't really a workaholic then. At that time, it was for survival, living on my own. I enjoyed that I was paying my own way and felt good about that, and I was being of service. I had fun with the other employees. I also had hours which suited me better than my previous school and nine-to-five schedule. When I talk about becoming a workaholic, it is immersion in work that was a distraction from my true self, which I fell into.

When I met my husband, I was just about finished with my college degree. There had been a long, slow process of working full-time, taking classes at night, and doing homework. My grades were so much better than the first time around. This was a self-esteem booster. I was doing it because I wanted to. I still consider my college degree one of my greatest achievements, since it took twelve calendar years from start to finish. The degree program that I started in, Media Communications, was so exciting with a Media focus. Back then, I wanted to be a journalist or TV newscaster. By the time I was finishing, though, the program had changed to Communication Arts. I still love and reflect on all the learning I got in college, especially from one teacher in particular who was always expanding my view of the world. When I finally graduated, it felt so strange to be at a point where I would have no commitment of trying to finish classes and do homework nights and weekends. For the first time since early childhood, I would have extra time on my hands.

I did not have the ability to see that as a positive thing, nor the ability to let my true self step forward and fill that time. Don't get me wrong, I knew my skills, and had much knowledge from all the jobs and schooling I had under my belt. I took pride in my accomplishments. Still, I didn't know how to step out of the box and feel into what I really wanted to be "when I grow up."

One thing I did know was that I wanted money. I wanted out of the hardship that I felt had been most of my life, and I felt money could solve it. So when my fiancé's mom suggested I get into real estate with her, I jumped in. The thing that attracted me to it the most was that there was no ceiling. I could be my own boss, and help others at the same time. My results would be my own. I made a good decision entering the field, but I didn't yet have what they now call life balance. My first commission was earned on us buying our own home. This was also my fiancé's mom's suggestion; I am so grateful to her for that and many other things. Then I began selling real estate part-time at night and on the weekends. My fiancé and I had full-time salaried jobs. We had dependable income, health insurance, and fixed expenses for the most part. However, due to having different money mentalities, I again felt that I was the one who had to change, I had a lack and scarcity vibe and he was showing me how to live. We loved each other and saw the best in each other. At this time, I still thought that someone else had the answers for me and I needed to fix myself. It was truly a great time in our lives. However, looking back, there was always this codependent way of mine that made me acquiesce on some important things when it became too difficult to discuss or find compromise. The outcome wasn't compromise. It was more like giving up instead of calmly telling the truth about how I really felt, since it might shake up the relationship completely, and that would have been the worst thing I could dream of. I see now that I would manipulate the situation by agreeing, deciding to change myself; I felt I was doing some big favor, when all I was doing was avoiding my truth and sabotaging us both. I still can't believe I didn't know it all along, but I would subconsciously assume any negative consequences of whatever actions I took that I truly didn't want to take were his fault, since I had chosen his needs over my own. I changed my mind, and my actions, to agree with him. I thought I had done my very best to discuss it and I had no other choice. Over time, stuffing yourself into the relationship by making choices against yourself becomes a habit, and then you just end up with more and more evidence to support that it is the other person causing you to choose them over yourself.

I began making real estate sales slowly but surely while also working at my full-time job. I helped first-time buyers get into their first house, condo, or multi-unit. I loved it! They were pleased with my work too, as I learned over the years when they called me back to assist them with their next move and recommended me to others. I remember diving into creating my own follow-up systems and learning as much as I could about real estate. Some of the other agents in the area didn't treat me well until I started getting listings. This just drove me harder. I became obsessed with succeeding. I made my clients happy and I felt great accomplishment each time.

I remember two specific events during my initial three-year part-time real estate career that pointed to my obsession. One incident was when I was driving home late at night, tired, and went right through a red light because I wasn't really aware of it. I knew that something bigger was wrong with that, but I just kept on. I also remember calling other agencies leaving messages to check on properties and set up showings one night at almost midnight, and my husband saying "What the hell are you doing? This is nuts!" All this really did at the time was convince me that I needed to quit my job and dedicate myself completely. I waited until our big project at my full-time job ended, then I jumped ship.

I will never forget my first full-time day in real estate. It was April Fool's Day, which was a Saturday that year, the day after my last day at my corporate job. On

Monday when my husband left for work at the usual seven a.m., I was on my own and self employed. I had finally arrived, my dream job. What happened after that was six years of ever-increasing distraction in the form of work. Oh, my lessons were there for me throughout, but I wasn't getting them. I made an income and sold a lot of houses, but still couldn't find my elusive, overall, deep happiness. I enjoyed the clients whom I connected with on a personal (and what I now see as spiritual) level. That was the best part. Of course, I liked the paychecks, the other reward for my effort, and the challenging and detailed work itself. If I could make enough money and become successful enough, it would make my problems go away, including my differences with my husband over money. However, the falsity of the situation was that what I was really *driven* to was to get away from the nagging feeling that I wasn't good enough. I was proving myself again. We bought a new house and new cars. I was spending on my business, my "professional" wardrobe, trainings, conventions, more systems and marketing tricks. I also had many assistants. There were eleven assistants in total. I realize now that my relationship issues were being tested, and I kept failing. I had a vision, which I communicated when I hired them, which they seemed to buy into, but it just never worked out. None of them got to the level of supporting me and taking the administrative reins to make me more productive. I was working to pay both of us, and yet I did not have the self-worth to find the right talent and hold them accountable. I had to fire a few. The others quit. It hurt me deeply, because I had to start over each time, and I was already working so hard. The last one got her real estate license behind my back, and that was it. I gave up. I stopped reporting to the office and moved my office to our house.

Coincidentally, through most of my workaholic phase, I had a lot of physical pain: lower back spasms, digestive issues, pinched nerves and immobility caused by neck and shoulder pain, and sciatic pain. I could no longer do all the physical exercise that I truly love, and I was sad about it. It is so interesting now to be able to see clearly how I was limiting myself, keeping myself in the distraction of work. There was a never-ending supply of work. I was a self-employed salesperson. Working from home without an assistant was quite eye opening. It became obvious very quickly that I could get certain things done faster myself, and I didn't have to carry so much back and forth to the office. I still worked too much, but I began to think about myself and what I was missing. I was burned out. However, without the constant trying to find and train the right employee, there was a little less stress. I suddenly realized that six years had passed since I went into real estate full time, I was thirty-nine years old, and it seemed I had been thrown off the hamster wheel of life by a slap in the face from fate, the last assistant quitting. My relationship with my husband at home was not going well, and the money was not flowing in enough abundance for both of us to have what we wanted. Truly, it was the beginning of my awakening from the mental fog that had followed me for so long.

Chapter Six
Opening Up to Others Again

Once I started working from home and slowed the breakneck pace for the first time, I noticed something quite profound. I had some major problems and I didn't understand why. I thought I had worked as hard as a person could to please my clients, please my husband, please my family, and make money. I began to wonder how I had ended up here. Why was it that all my hard work hadn't paid off? Why was it that I could not make enough money to keep my husband and me from fighting over it? Why was it that no matter how much I thought I wanted more closeness with others, and more freedom to be myself, that maybe I didn't really know who I was? Maybe no one else did either? I tried to talk to my husband about our money situation. I was so frustrated that we were not getting ahead, because I had been working so hard. We were not able to have any fruitful conversations. In fact, it seemed everything was the other person's fault. Things got worse very quickly, and I felt completely helpless and hopeless to work with my husband to fix anything. The only thing that I accomplished by trying to work together to solve our problems was to push him away. I felt alone, hopeless, and physically unhealthy.

I began to seek out new friendships and activities to fulfill my need for positive contact and something better than I had been experiencing. I still enjoyed real estate and working with my clients. Whenever I was not working, though, the sadness and frustration crept back into my psyche. I would talk to myself about how I needed to start taking care of myself and my own goals. I had to figure out who I was and be able to communicate that to my husband, or at least become it and *then* find a way to explain it. I knew that things were not right between us, but I did not have the ability to talk about it without us fighting. I was feeling resentful again.

I joined a small weekly astrology class, invited by a friend. It seemed like a good idea. I had always loved reading the descriptions of Scorpio, my sign, and the other sun signs as they related to me and my loved ones. And the books that described someone born on a certain birthday. This class was my first true venture into the holistic world. I had always been attracted to subjects such as Tarot cards, Ouija boards, séances, and mysteries. People have reminded me that I did consider myself psychic before this, based simply on the many indisputable coincidences, dreams and predictions that had happened to me, although they were not very frequent. The astrology class was so exciting for me. Within a month or so I had scheduled a full astrological birth chart reading with the teacher to find out more about the subject of astrology and about myself.

I will never forget what happened that day of my reading. She sat across from me and went over my chart by explaining the way the planets were aligned at the time I was born, and how they related to my personality, family, relationships, history, and more. I remember being completely dumbfounded and amazed. This person, who was truly just an acquaintance at that point, seemed to understand me better than anyone had in my whole life. She spoke of my greatest challenges, frustrations, joys, and inspirations. The best part was that she spoke of my natural psychic and counseling abilities, and she said, "You are a medium." I knew what a medium was. In fact, I was watching them on TV and was fascinated. Another thing I remember quite clearly was that she said the greatest medicine for me to give myself was to play, and I already knew that was something I loved.

It took several days to absorb it all, and I listened to the tape recording of the reading several times. I remember telling my husband that she said I was a medium and I knew she was right. I had connected with the spirits of my deceased loved ones before, and he and I had even experienced it together. I cried after I told him, and when he asked why, I said I was scared because I didn't want to be on TV, and I didn't want to see gory murder scenes. I was very pleased, though, that I had a reason to delve deeper into the psychic world.

I was recommended to a medium teacher, signed up for her beginners' class later that year, and read her book in the meantime. It was only shortly before that when I had begun reading something other than real estate news. I also took up yoga, despite my physical pain. I thought I had a permanently bad back. My mom came to visit a couple of months after my astrology reading, and right before she left, she said "What you need is yoga." I took her advice and delved into yoga with an eager spirit. My body did not follow as quickly. The next thing I knew I was sweating on a yoga mat in hot power yoga, silently cursing my inadequacy.

I had been a gymnast. I could do splits, aerials, and back tucks, I had been flexible and powerful. This was not the body I had now. I cried for the whole first ten classes or so. Luckily, everyone was so sweaty and the music and teacher were loud enough that no one noticed. I heard later that the positions of yoga practice encourage a lot of stuck energy out of the joints and hips and everywhere, and this can feel emotional as it comes up for release. Yoga was a great new friend, as frustrating as it was. I always felt better after I went. I kept this up two to three times a week for many months. My strength and flexibility were coming back, and it was helping my bad back. People in the class were friendly but everyone pretty much was deep in their own yoga journey. I remember sometimes, as I was leaving for yoga, my husband and I would be fighting. I was watching the clock because I had to get to the class. It would end with him yelling, "Fine, go ahead, go to yoga!" I made the choice each time to leave him in that moment and go to yoga. It was a huge challenge, because I wanted to resolve our troubles, but I knew yoga was one of the only things going right in my personal life. Those classes were the hardest. My strength was not there on those days. But my spirit was awakening and my body was feeling better again. I was choosing me.

Things between my husband and me were at their worst. I begged him to go to counseling with me. I spent more time with friends, both old and new. While I said I wanted it, and my husband also supported me and wanted it for me, truly I was afraid of having deep close friends again, because of some terrible experiences I'd had with friendships ending. Interestingly enough, the astrology reading had helped make sense of this too. My healing gifts are centered around helping those in transition. Many people had come and gone in my life and I would be devastated when I lost them. I know now that they were only in my life for a reason and a season as they say. I began to tell someone else about what was going on at home, instead of keeping everything to myself, trying to deal with and fix everything while pretending it was all good on the surface. I truly was in denial. Even as I spoke of the dysfunction, I knew that I was trying to get out of it for the first time by telling someone. Previously, I operated from a pattern of protecting myself and my relationship with my husband from what others might think, along with protecting my identity this way, since I felt I could get through anything and I was sure it would all work out. I knew deep inside that the dynamic was not right. However I did not want anyone to know, including myself, so I did not speak of it. I started skipping his hockey games, to which I had gone for many years. They were late at night, so it had been pretty easy; I would just bring my work. I wanted him to start appreciating me and doing more for me. I began to discuss with my close friends my greater dissatisfactions with my life, and what I found was that this vulnerability I was sharing was received with gentleness and support. Better yet, I was feeling more like I could have a friend again. Most importantly, I was allowing myself to know and hear that my relationship troubles were pretty big. What I still did not see at this time was that I was still in the pattern of the victim.

Chapter Seven
Lessons, Lessons, Lessons

I can sum up most of my lessons with the word *reaction*. I started realizing that life was offering me lessons, instead of hard knocks, and I went back to therapy as my marriage was falling apart. I began traveling the road of my awakening from my negative patterns. Through the books I was reading and the classes I was taking, I began to learn that my own mental and emotional health was tied to my reactions. In other words, there was no need to react negatively or defensively to something that was happening to me, that someone was supposedly doing to me, saying to me, or saying about me, no matter what it was. This was the greatest challenge I had ever considered. As I pondered it, I realized that in the past, after a difficult conversation or event, I would be left thinking of what I "should have said." And what I should have said was actually falsely motivated by my belief that the other person needed more evidence to realize that I had my reasons or I had my rights, because they weren't talking to me with compassion, or they had no consideration for my position. Everything involved the other person. I realized that I was always thinking of things as evidence that I was right and "they" were wrong.

It was as if my actions held a certain concern behind them, at all times, about what others thought, or what they would think. Even though I would always claim to do what I wanted, there was an inherent quality of having to prove that I had justification, research, or validation to support myself in my decisions and actions. Who did I need to have that for? Why did I need to make sure that what I did was okay? Most of this, of course, happened with my husband. We were not getting along, and we wanted to so badly. I wanted to talk it out. I wanted to fix it. I always knew I was strong and could tackle anything, and I thought he was too. But every time I tried to talk, I lost the argument. Even if my reason won the argument, I still lost, because we could not work it out.

This was when I learned about what they call codependency, starting with a book my therapist gave me, and I learned that the greatest downside of being codependent is that you are actually being controlling. You are focused on another person and what they should do, what they need to do, how they need to pay attention to what you think they should, or make changes, or get on board with you and your plan. Or you're taking care of them. Helping them. Enabling them, in many cases. I remember spending time thinking about how I could try this or try that with my husband. I would think about what I would say, how what I tried before didn't work, and therefore I had to try this next thing. Expecting, knowing, that there would be an argument. See, that was the lesson. My expectation of a fight made it so. I thought my entire focus was about how I could find a way for us to work on our major problems, together. Yet I was actually sabotaging my own life by focusing on someone else.

Around this time I also became interested in and started to learn about the Law of Attraction, and I was enlightened as to how many things were, in fact, beliefs I had about the "way things are." I also noticed that the harder I tried, the harder I fell. I learned that I was "resisting." The Law of Attraction says that whatever we focus on, we get. As an example, I thought that the reason I had some crazy situations happen during my life was because I was the kind of person that could get through it. You know, God only gives you what you can handle? Now I was realizing that I could be drawing more crazy situations to myself by thinking that way. I began to choose thoughts about what I wanted instead of noticing what was wrong or hard.

As I played with my psychic, mediumistic, and hands-on healing abilities and gifts, I brought healing to myself. I was quite amused and also very nervous about it in the beginning, as it was all unfamiliar, and there were a lot of new things to know, ways of doing the psychic thing properly, as every psychic and teacher I met would explain. It was a whole new world. One thing was sure, a *big* lesson: I had these gifts and they weren't going away. I felt inspired to find a way to use them, develop them, and talk about them. In the beginning I also felt I had to do this without calling extra attention to myself, or ridicule. I was aware of the powerful energy of the naysayers, still in fear of what others thought. However I began to feel so much more normal and peaceful as I explored it. The experiences that would happen when I used my gifts were extremely fulfilling. It was not at all because it seemed I could do magic—that was just the childhood dream. The bigger fulfillment was the healing that it brought to myself and others. I started to develop a backbone. Not a defensive strength or a greater capacity to fight. Instead, a stronger sense of something that was truly me, some-thing I loved about myself that was not going anywhere. I was OK. In fact, I saw my gifts developing and becom-ing stronger and better. I had something in my life that was very good and made me feel happy and healthy and could even bring in money too. I took every opportunity I could to experience more of it, even though my husband, when we fought, would make fun of me about it, when I spoke of signs, symbolism, and my future. He could hurt me, but he couldn't take it away. I had a core. I had something unfolding for me that was bigger than anything I had ever experienced. It put my life in perspective. It seemed to explain why I had received so many lessons. I was extremely intuitive and I now realize I had a lot of extra feelings and thoughts because of it my whole life, and that is why I felt crazy. I *was* different. I was more psychic than most people.

I truly believe that people like me, who have to learn not to give too much and learn to focus on themselves more than others, are healers. That's what I call us. We go through some extremely tough things, that build our strength, our character, and most of all, our compassion. I had *zero* compassion for my husband during this time of lessons. Everything he did felt like it was against me, to me, or to spite me. I remember coming home and just dreading walking into my own house because he was there, and I was sure he felt the same. I know many of you reading this know exactly what I am talking about. There is hardly a worse feeling than not wanting to be in the same house with the person you live with. I had no words that worked, no tools. My love for him could not be expressed in a way that helped. It's like our reactions and our egos were battling a war and we as our true selves were helpless to transcend them. The best I could do at the time was try a new approach, and cry it all out as he got increasingly more angry. I even tried getting angry back. That was all very ugly. I really don't know if I would take it all back if I could. We knew, even then, that we didn't really want to treat each other that way. However we had no other skills to get through it. We were both reacting. We were both learning lessons. I didn't see it that way most of the time. Most of the time I was just praying and hoping and preparing for a breakthrough. The moment the interaction went south, I was fit to be tied. I was helpless, hopeless, and spent. I think about all the people who went their separate ways in that kind of anger and disconnection from each other, while truly deep down desiring the relationship very much. It's no wonder when we leave one relationship we tend to end up down the road with the same relationship lessons, only with a different person. The reactions and predispositions that I began to see in myself during this time, I had only begun to conquer. The first step is awareness, as they say. The changing of one's own behavior, when the other person seems most certainly wrong, and trying to harm us unnecessarily, is the harder part.

That is the lesson for me, for us, for you. You are choosing. Each moment, each word that comes out of your mouth, you are choosing. Each action, you are choosing. Each thought, you are choosing. When you begin to see that it's futile to blame and say that it's because of someone else, you are beginning to move toward the life you truly want. We can all point to why we "had to" or why they "made us," but truly we choose our thoughts, our reactions, and our life, moment by moment. Take any story of triumph over adversity and you will hear the same thing—I wasn't going to let it stop me. Circumstance is only one factor in life. What we do with ourselves in each moment is all about choice.

Chapter Eight
Heart Broken Open

How does one describe a broken heart? To me, it is the deepest human emotion there is. I was introduced to a new concept of a broken heart by a book I read called *Shambhala: The Sacred Path of the Warrior* by Chögyam Trungpa. It is the concept that when one truly looks at something beautiful like a flower, or the ocean, it breaks your heart. The beauty in the world is so powerful that everything breaks your heart. One could live as if their heart is already broken, raw, and beautiful, completely vulnerable, and yet open and unable to have your heart broken because it's already broken. I have had my heart broken before. But this time, it was by my husband, whom I had intended to be with, in faithful, mutual love, for the rest of my life. I desired to fix the relationship, more than anything else at that point in my life, even though it was a difficult love at the time.

My heart was so broken, in just one instant, when I asked him the question, already knowing the answer. He confirmed it: he was having an affair. My mind wanted to know how I could have been fooled. Who was this liar? My heart wanted to know how it would ever feel whole enough to love again. There was such a pain in my heart, in my physical chest. I knew I had never felt that depth of pain before. It seemed to travel through me, so deeply, as if all the way to the center of the Earth. But wait, pain and pleasure are so close in nature. Have you ever noticed that the cries of pain are similar to the cries of passion? I remember my heart breaking then as a beautiful thing now, if you can believe that. It sent me down the path that I cherish the most, so far. It caused me to tackle true forgiveness. It caused me to look at myself. It caused me to get out of denial and see just what had been going on with me all my life.

I cried and grieved. I grieved for the love that was lost. I grieved for my stupidity and humiliation. For having worked so hard and yet losing the thing that meant the most. I grieved for the stigma of divorce, for the dream many little girls share...of being a princess and living happily ever after. I grieved for our shared memories, tarnished forever.

Somewhere in those depths, though, I found something else even more resonant. It's the only thing that is there, in that darkest place of a broken heart. It is the nothing. The nothing which is the everything from which we all came, the nothing from which there is no escape. The nothing we return to when we take our last breath. The stillness, the silence. I believe we all know deep inside that this entire life is just born of nothing, that birth itself is a complete and total miracle. That the meaning of life is found here, in life itself. The nothing is a place where a caterpillar becomes imaginal cells and completely dissolves itself within the cocoon, re-emerging as a butterfly after the miracle of transformation which science can only point to. Life is only an unfolding story, or drama if you will, of us in relation to the "others" we have brought into our lives or were born into life with. Some people's "others" are less people, and more objects. Even those attached to objects more than people know the objects are not the deepest thing, are not the true reality but just there for us to play with in order to derive meaning and happiness. In the end, won't we all be dead? You can't take it with you, as they say. This life is just an illusion. I believe when your heart is broken, your heart is broken open. You go to the depths and wonder what the hell is there, and what's it all for. It must be a joke. It is!

Now I'm not saying that I knew all this at that moment. At that moment, it was the beginning of a long road out of that darkness and pain, that nothing, that confusion. Every moment and every step I took after my heart broke open, I was asking myself what was it all for. What did I really want? What was important? What is anything worth? How much strength does it take to live in this world? Who is in charge of my life if not me? How did I get here, in this mess? Dear God, why?

Chapter Nine
Spiritual Path

So now I get all weird on you and talk about my spiritual path. But what is a spiritual path? I think that's what the continuing question is. My own definition of a spiritual path is really what this whole book is about. There is a bigger picture, no? If there is not, then why are we here? Is it just to suffer these confining human conditions that I've been describing, following carrots all our lives only to die without feeling like we "did it right"? Perhaps there is no bigger picture. No Maker, no Judgment Day. Who is watching you and me, besides ourselves and each other? Surely there is someone making bad things happen to us. We would never choose it. Or would we?

Day by day, after what felt like my world collapsing, I began to look at my own behavior. I went through an entire range of emotions over everything that had happened, and tried to sort them out somehow. I had by this time begun to explore my spiritual gifts, the laws of the universe, and spent some serious time on a yoga mat. I began to see those who supposedly caused my pain as just pawns in the story of my life. The emotions that I was "made" to feel, the things that happened: how can I let these be the truth of my life? I certainly would not agree that I was choosing everything that had happened. How had I let everything outside of me control my life? There must be a way that all of this is being created, I thought, and I began to search for it. What was my part? I had to get to the bottom of it.

Right after the affair came to light, my husband and I had a conversation, the nature of which we could have had all along if we hadn't both been in defense, reaction, and ego with each other. We spoke of the way we felt about each other and what had changed over the years from a place of wanting answers, without fighting, and knowing that nothing mattered, since our relationship was technically over. Once we had this conversation, a cloud was lifted, the affair was over, and we were back in sync just as we had been when we met. This part, we cannot explain. It just was. Sometimes I think it is proof of what love really is, when I think about the horrible things we said and did to each other, and how it can feel as if it's all just gone, in the past, like those things never happened. We both felt that these were only lessons to enhance us.

I began to take some true control in my life. The real estate market was taking a turn for the worse. I knew that we needed to sell our house, and it suddenly did not matter what kind of pressure, from who, or how many reasons not to there were coming at me. There was no doubt in my mind and I was clear about it. My happiness, security, the future of our relationship, if there was truly going to be one, was on the line, and was more important than a big, beautiful house that we had purchased from a sense of obligation to the path we had been on. This wasn't easy by any means, to say goodbye to the house. I loved it and what it represented. It would not be easy to relocate with two dogs and not a lot of cash. I was, however, ready to let go of whatever was not serving me. This is a phrase that became so close to my heart, "letting go of what's not serving me." I did this a lot at that time; however it was far from a dominating experience. It was gut-wrenching at worst, and bittersweet at best. Familiarity is so hard to let go of. Familiarity gives a sense of safety. The power to be in control and choose my own life was growing every time I let go of the familiar in favor of a step toward something unknown that I knew felt even more right. It was a completely different power than anything I'd ever felt. It was not physical, it was not calculated, or vengeful, it was not elation. It was pure and simple energetic power. The kind that makes you feel as though there *is*, indeed, a reason for being here. The kind that makes you take a deep breath because something has been lifted that you hadn't realized you'd been carrying all along.

Things began to have a different meaning. They still had the same faces and qualities, they still caused me the "same shit, different day," as they say. I hadn't changed very much. But something within me, something beyond me, was starting to help me, giving me strength. I have to say here that it is not unlike the faith that serves many devout Christians, Catholics, or AA members. I had not felt it previously, though. Religion to me had been a roller-coaster ride. Born Protestant, changed to Catholic after my parents split, and then to Episcopal when I moved back with my dad. I did not enjoy the Catholic church at all. My mom told me that the priests were celibate, but something inside me was screaming that was impossible, it wasn't right. I refused to receive Catholic confirmation as a teenager, even though I went through the class, and God knows where the nerve came from to do that, but this newfound power was the exact same kind. A knowing, something within myself that no one could change. It was my truth. Saying no to something that I knew I had to say no to, or at least *begin* trying to say no to, knowing that it was imperative that there be success. No going back. I did not want my previous life anymore, where things happened to me.

This was not about control. Not about not being blindsided. It was about having been completely blind. Not seeing that I was not living for me, I was living for an image of me that, no matter where it had come from, I had bought into.

It was about the relationship between myself and myself. There were certain things that were becoming clear to me. With each step, each day, I was seeing with new eyes: How did I get here? Why do I do things this way? How can any of these patterns possibly be changed, the ones that don't feel good, anyway? From the big details to the small, I couldn't change it all in the blink of an eye. But I could listen to myself first. Myself was still quite confused and torn between "standing up for myself" and "putting up with it" at this time. They seemed to be the only two options. Once I would decide between the two, and you guessed it, putting up with it was going mostly out the window, next would come the insanity of torturing myself about how I would do it. What would I say, how would that go, what would happen if someone didn't agree with what I felt was best for me and I had to make even tougher decisions? I have to say that at this time, while it was very painful in the aftermath of losing trust in my husband, my workaholic dreams, and my house, I was climbing out of a hole and that part felt great. I was no longer spinning out of control wondering which way life would take me. I was tackling my life with a newfound power, the power of knowing that all that really mattered in the end is my life experience, what I was giving *to* life, what it was giving me. I was here for a reason—and the reason is my life itself.

Although I began working with my psychic gifts many months before, my heart breaking was indeed, my spiritual awakening, as I call it. It was just like a lightning bolt of change. Therefore, it was the moment I set foot upon my spiritual path. Before that, I didn't understand the gift of my own life, I just went about it. Now I knew there was indeed a power greater than myself, something I could not control, but something that did not control me, either. It was a power that was there for me. For everyone else too. The power of good. The power of Spirit. The power of this life as a journey for human happiness and beauty. God, if you like. Doesn't matter what you call it.

Chapter Ten
Tearing Myself from "Other"

Who am I? What do I want? Some space opened up in my consciousness and began to grow. It became important to talk to myself, to stop looking out at life as if it was my enemy, my challenge, or my muck to wade through. Why don't I look at what is here *for* me, I thought, versus what does not feel right for me? This was the question I dared to ask, and I answered it with reflection on a daily basis. This was not a practice, per se, as one might think of purposely doing meditation. In fact, I resisted meditation. These concepts that were coming into me were happening as if my mind was unfolding, unraveling. It wasn't something I was purposely doing, except in each moment of looking at my thoughts and my reality in a different way, based on the new concepts that had taken root. Instead, it was happening just as part of the moment-to-moment tapestry that was my life. Something was pushing me from beyond myself, not to define myself, but to use myself. A knowing so deep it makes you feel as if someone else is talking to you. A strange concept. However, if, indeed this life was for living, for my happiness, then it did seem pertinent for me to start addressing what I was doing that I liked, and what was going on that I didn't like.

Often I found myself previously in an inner turmoil, and inner fury, that sounded something like this: "What if they do this to me? What if they say that to me? What if this happens? What will I do?" More like worry. Now the inner thoughts were changing to something more like "I wonder if I've always done that because I like it, or because I am trying to make someone else happy?" and "Perhaps my love of this is not just because it makes me feel better when I feel beat up by life, but because I really love it and want it in my life all the time." Then the questions got harder. The thoughts would ask me whether I was willing to live with something or not. They would ask me how long I was going to deny something before I faced it. They asked me why I always repeated thinking some negative thing about myself.

As I continued with my spiritual gifts, using them for intuitive readings and healings, I realized that it felt so right for me, and it helped me to help others this way.

I started to let my judgment of being different and being psychic fall away. I began to notice what others' energy felt like, and what mine felt like, while doing readings and healings. I noticed that I felt their energy within me, but that I could be aware of the difference between theirs and mine. The more intuitive I became, with practice, the more I asked myself what my preferences in life really were, and what I wanted to spend my precious time doing. Feeling into others, I felt the troubles, the pain, the blocks that were familiar to me in my own life, but now I was describing them, shedding light on them. Those whom I worked with felt heard, and they could understand the patterns because of course they wanted out of them too. They were shifted and healed by becoming more aware of things when I validated it as a psychic, and they could move in a different direction.

I was still very much involved in reacting to things, and in my ego. These two words, *reaction* and *ego*, to me describe the innate human pull to put what's around you, especially other people, front and center. The opposite is to put front and center the light- and space-filled awareness of the miracle of yourself as a unique and infinite being in that moment—the observer, the recipient of the magic called life. I was beginning to see that right versus wrong and good versus bad were not helpful. They were simply judgments that kept me locked in thinking "what if" and trying to decide what to do. My husband and I fell back into our negative patterns with each other after we moved and sold the house. The marriage was not working, for either of us. It seemed all we did was hurt each other. We went to couples' therapy and individual therapy, and while we learned a lot, we kept pushing each other's buttons the wrong way, and I kept coming up against his anger. This made me so mad! Our therapist suggested medication for him. This made me happy at first, as I felt most of the trouble would be solved by this. It was a roller coaster. I see now that my victim pattern was asking for these kinds of validations. There was no doubt that we had a strong and deep connection, what I always called a soul-mate connection, but it just wasn't working. We were in couples' therapy and individual therapy and yet we were both unable to discover compassion for and acceptance of the other's issues. We still kept pointing to the other as the problem. I decided to take mercy on us both and leave him. It wasn't a fresh idea. We had said it to each other many times already. However, it was the hardest thing I had ever done in my entire life. I knew neither of us really wanted that. I desperately wanted the relationship to work.

As I made this decision to put us both out of our misery, I kept chanting the Serenity Prayer to ensure myself I was doing the right thing. Until that day I never really paid much attention to it. I had explored Alanon briefly during this time, which was very helpful, and someone gave me a little coin with the Serenity Prayer. "God grant me the *serenity* to accept the things I cannot change, *courage* to change the things I can, and *wisdom* to know the difference." I decided I was going to change the only thing I could. I knew the difference this time. I was tearing myself from other. I looked at my life from the perspective of what's right for me. If I do what's right for me, it will be right for everyone around me. My spiritual path. So I quickly found an apartment, and it was less than twenty-four hours before the next moment of impasse between us. He repeated "Why don't you just leave?" and this time I said, "Okay, I'm leaving." And I began packing.

I was afraid to tell him, I was afraid he would be the most angry yet when I told him. He had also recently begun a new medication for a new diagnosis. I read up on the diagnosis. I asked myself if I should stay and work through it. But I was leaving the misery and the pain that I knew neither of us deserved or had any power to overcome at that time. I knew one thing, that this was not a life I could live one more day. What I have learned about anger since, is that being someone who many say has a very open and loving heart, I detested anger itself. I often suppressed my own, and I often reverted to a childlike victim in the face of someone else's anger at me. I have learned to express my anger, or at least, become friendly with it, and therefore I'm not so scared of it coming at me either. It is simply an emotion, and all emotions flow through human beings. I believe resisting them creates energetic blocks and patterns of self-sabotage, as we deny ourselves and others' true nature as humans. And I believe the Universe keeps sending us what we have not accepted, until we finally allow and accept it within ourselves and stop labeling and rejecting it as if we would never be that. Of course it seems appropriate to learn to temper oneself so as not to hurt others unintentionally. But sometimes, we just fire our anger directly at another person. There are many ways to deal with anger that are healthy. At this time my husband and I could not find any.

More recently, it became clear that our own interactions with each other built up so much mutual resentment. We were two smart, strong, and passionate people working hard to blame the other for their problems and avoid being truly vulnerable and intimate. His "mental illness" is no more, in fact never was. It was something we both subscribed to, as it seemed to be an answer to help us. We are each who we are. Each of us can and will decide his or her own path day by day.

In contemplating the finality of leaving, I was walking away from the love of my life, the one I had invested in, even if he hated me for the rest of my life, and never spoke to me again. I had to do it for both of us. "God grant me the courage to change the things I can." At first, he talked to those who were on his side, and began to discuss protecting himself from me financially. He told me I was weak. A quitter. It didn't stop me.

Then, instead, as the few days left before I moved went by, I found him sharing his thoughts and his heart. In the early morning hours before I moved out, just a few days later, lying in bed together, there was a bottom. We both felt it, and he put words to it. Things would never be the same. I had created a major change in the situation. The words soothed my soul. It was just like when I swam as a little girl. The bottom was always there and when I reached it, a beautiful moment of weight-lessness overcame me as I softly bounced up. This time my beloved was with me and it was beautiful.

Next, I found myself in my new apartment, in complete silence, a gorgeous and giant silence that expanded me in all directions. I did not turn on the TV or radio for a week. In the meantime, my beloved Michael's heart broke open just as mine had only a year before. He suddenly knew what he truly felt because he couldn't help but feel it. He spoke and wrote of such beautiful feelings, love, and purpose, and instead of the raw ending I was completely committed to facing, his words made sense of our entire time together, and he showed me the deep loving person I had married, and more. He was supporting me in leaving him, and in all the changes I was making for myself. He began to claim his own spiritual gifts too and is one of the most spiritual people I've been blessed to have in my life.

The next thing that happened was that we got divorced. But we were still a couple. Shocking to some, but I was not afraid of being different anymore. It was a boundary. I was setting boundaries through separation and divorce. That was the only way I could set them at the time, I did not yet have the personal power to navigate things any other way. There was too much "other" and not enough "myself." This was because I was codependent. Worrying about the other person more than myself, and not in a good way. I wasn't that strong yet. Leaving made me so much stronger. I couldn't believe I had done it and my friends couldn't either; they knew I loved him and wanted to stay together. And just as when I left him, divorcing him was for both of us, I desperately wanted to end our money fights and I knew that we deserved better. He started his own business during this time with my full support and became successful with it and with managing money. We are all different—no one is better. The choices we, and all people make, are right for them at the time. At that time I was working on *boundaries*.

When do I say no? How do I say no? How can I let someone down, when I was so good at doing everything to avoid it? This was my work. The outcomes of our choices are simply that...there is no going back and we live our life day by day.

I began exploring many facets of my consciousness. There were pivotal books and classes. I also began to delve into other areas of real estate for my good clients, such as rentals and commercial. Instead of trying to please every client who came my way, I began to work harder for the few that I clicked with, saying no to the matches that weren't right. I was learning that my giving, my ability to feel the other without even trying, was misplaced energy for me if it were not the right people. Giving more and more readings, I felt everything, and I gave everything I could to help those I read for. I began to be sure to charge money for these services. It was awesome to me, the ability I had when I sat to do a reading. Now I was learning to be able to discern with that gift and know what was me and what was "other." I was tearing myself from other in every way.

I was not becoming more of an individual, though; it seemed that would be going backward. Instead I was offering myself where I felt best matched, by noticing which energy matched and which didn't. Of course, the best practice was with my husband. I had spent so long inadvertently intuiting what he would do, say, what he felt, how to avoid things or manipulate things to feel safe, be safe, and protect myself. Now I was finding the courage to stop and feel: what was right for me? I was begging and praying for the words to come to make it clear to him, when I was forced to stand up for what was right for me when we disagreed. For a while I avoided discussing certain things, not knowing it was because of my fear of ending up with irreconcilable differences. In the end, as I believe the natural ways of the universe is constantly arranging for us, everything comes to a head; I painfully yet gratefully traverse each challenge, knowing the gift of the situation is surely waiting for me around the next bend, as following my inner GPS is the only way to go. We can only see the road a little bit in front of us. That's the magic of life, that's the game. I've heard that many people have been asked if they would like to know how their life would go if they could, and most say no.

As time goes on, having to stand up for myself comes along much less often. Not only is it easier for me to look into myself and speak up about what I want and need, but I also find that life has begun to listen to my thoughts, dreams, and desires as I move toward them and things just aren't as volatile. I may die tomorrow, but I am living for myself, and I enjoy the connection with those I love more than I ever have at the same time. It's a new direction, an energy, a power of the individual soul as it grows to fulfill itself in the form of a human life and all the lives that it touches. I believe each of us has many gifts, in fact the capacity for every gift, the greatest of them being the uniqueness that we each are, with our mixture of gifts and personality. Certainly we are not all born with the same strength of gifts in every area. This is why the tapestry of life is like an interaction of these gifts. It feels good to give. It feels good to receive. It feels good to interact with all situations from a place of safety, knowing that my best friend is me. If I follow her, things will always be better than they were before, when I didn't know who she was. I've also learned that I can follow myself without having to stand up for myself. Just knowing that everything is a choice, means I don't always have to say or announce what I don't agree with. Instead of avoiding a subject as I may have done out of fear, now if the subject is not brought up it's because it didn't need to be. There's less anxiety and anticipation.

Chapter Eleven
Learning to Go Within

What happened next was that I began to discern the differences between what I was feeling and what others were feeling, on a day-to-day basis. I had no idea I had been picking up so much all along. The way it began was that I would notice that I was having strong feelings about someone I cared about, someone very close to me. This had always happened, but I was noticing for the first time. I thought these were my thoughts. The thoughts I was having about them, though, felt strange! In fact they always had, now that I thought about it. For example, one of the first times I came to understand all this, was that I kept thinking about someone else's next birthday and how old they would be turning. I kept noticing this repeating thought and then saying to myself, "Why do I keep thinking this?" It seemed as if I was making something up about someone else, and I wondered why I would do that. Over and over I thought about it. Then I mentioned it to the person, which felt very strange to do, but it turned out that they were thinking over and over about the age they would be turning! I suddenly knew I had been picking up on their thought, a strong feeling in their energy. I found out how often this happened, because I started mentioning these thoughts to the people they were about, and it turned out that more and more, it was actually someone else's thoughts. Of course they noticed it was odd too, but being close to me, they already knew I was psychic by then. I would like to say here that I believe we are all psychic, picking up thoughts, feelings, and judgments from outside ourselves all the time that we think are ours. I think it's just louder for me than most people.

Then I began to think about how much of me was being used up with someone else's thoughts. How much of my energy was I spending on these thoughts that didn't belong to me? These thoughts didn't feel that great, because they always made me wonder why I was having them. Then I decided that it was appropriate just to send good intentions to the situation, and let it go. Move on to some thoughts and feelings of my own that needed to be processed.

Hey, wait a minute, what were my own thoughts and feelings? They felt different. They had more of a *Yes!*

DEAR GOD, WHY?

or a *No*! to them. I realized that I could tune in, tune myself like a radio, in a way, tune into the inside of me, ask myself what felt the most like my own, the best, the deepest. Pretty soon it began to be quite clear to me what was mine and what was not.

Here is an example of the ways I would be tested, and how I began to decide what to do with my energy and thoughts. I saw someone on a business purpose who had just lost someone suddenly, someone they were very close to. This death was hard on them and their life situation, very unexpected and unsettling. I gave of myself while I was with them. I cried for them and for the family. It was an especially tough spot for me because there was a business relationship, an overlying professional environment. And yet I was a medium, and I was being given the push to do some mediumship and they were open to it. It was also out of blue for me. I was just there to do business, not expecting strong emotions. Afterward I went on with my day, but my day wouldn't go on very easily. I couldn't stop thinking about it. I couldn't stop thinking about them, all the pain, all the reasons why it was so sad and so hard. And then suddenly, realizing I had lost control, I said out loud, "This is not mine! I don't have to feel this! I want this to go away now!" About a half hour later I realized it had gone away. I had trouble with having asked for it to go away, even though it was what I wanted and it had worked, because I felt bad for letting it go. I felt guilty somehow for just moving on so quickly, because it truly was sad. Then I remembered that if my life were to be my own, going in the direction that I choose for my greatest happiness, enjoying my work, play, and those around me, that this was indeed the right thing to do and I was glad to be discovering it. I really wasn't offering much to them by helping carry and promote the sadness. I needed to acknowledge the energy of their situation, ask and pray for its healing. I could do a reading. Beyond that, it was not my work or in my power to do anything else that would ease the stress, trauma, and pain that I could feel them going through. In fact, my belief is that adding my sadness to theirs would only intensify and give growth and power to that energy.

In such moments, I began to decide again and again to move on from sad thoughts about others with a newfound power, freedom, and gladness to be able to drop what didn't belong to me and focus on what did. I knew that sad things happen and will continue to happen in my own life and in the lives of those close to me, and I surely have had and will continue to have my share, and end up sharing in sad times with others. Just like the teachings of Abraham (of Abraham-Hicks Publications) I had been listening to had taught me, no amount of feeling bad can ever offer another any true help. Only feeling good, a "higher vibration," as Abraham calls it, can offer vibrational alignment with what is true and right for oneself, vibrating authenticity, giving that as an offering to others in the process. Have you ever known someone who was just pure and authentic in almost everything they did? I have. This is what someone in alignment with themselves offers. You never wonder where you stand with them, as you know they are nothing but honest.

There is so much I could write about here. So many things have happened that have taught me how to refocus, redirect, and recalibrate, in times of confusion, due to this learning to go within. It may sound complicated, but it's the easiest thing in the world. You just drop what isn't yours, and get on with your best self. Now, of course, you have loved ones you choose to help, and you choose to take on things for others, as they do for you. However, when you are in touch with your own thoughts and feelings and are clear about what they are, you are usually offering this help from a pure state of alignment with your own wants and needs. You are giving something that it is giving you a sort of pleasure to give, even if it's a really tough situation. You are choosing to give something, and it makes you feel right and in purpose to give it. No one is taking; they are just receiving, if they are able. It is simply a win-win. And remember, if everyone is always giving, there would not be enough people to receive that giving. We must also realize when we would need or want help, and know that we deserve to receive it and it doesn't make us weak. If everyone were in a state of alignment with their inner selves, then no one would have to worry about receiving anything that wasn't meant and gifted to them. We all need support and help sometimes. Giving and receiving it make people and relationships better, I believe.

You may say, as I did, "Well, what about the takers? What about the people who are just always pushing you to give more than you want, needing you, and making you feel as if you are a jerk for not doing what they say or giving them what they want?" Again, it is clear to me now that being in touch with one's own inner compass is the answer. If I am clear inside, within myself, what I want or don't want, need or don't need, feel good about or don't feel good about, then there is no drama. There is just me knowing and being my own friend, and stating the answers which "we" have agreed on. Makes me smile. I'm my own best friend. I have learned to say no.

There is complete and utter uncertainty in every day of this life. However, there is a beautiful gift in that, each moment is really all there is, and if we keep following our inner GPS, we will be where we are meant to be. No matter what that feels like, there will be that feeling of knowing you are there for and because of yourself and the divine plan for you. It's an energetic path. Which is not something someone decides. God is not a brain.

Chapter Twelve
Awakening to Higher Self

I change my mind all the time. It seems to go like this: I come to a new conclusion, whether it's related to what I do not want anymore or something I definitely want going forward. I get so excited about my revelations that it's as if I'm standing on a soap box when I tell others about it. I happily speak about what I have discovered and how I have changed my general paradigm of living. It is somewhat like rock climbing, though; where I have landed, my support to use to take a step higher. As I climb, I look back at that position and realize it is no longer supporting me in the next step. I have already made that climb. Those I have spoken to of my revelations may or may not be in my life anymore. They may or may not have been affected by what I've shared. But it's been my nature to share it. These life-altering "new" conclusions may have affected those I told by offering general inspirational energy I embodied as I was overcoming my challenge, the pure exhilaration of that, and that anything is possible. It may have affected them in a way that they resonated with, and they ended up adopting the new beliefs I embodied in that moment. It may have been a catalyst, where they may have decided something about themselves or something in their life that is the complete opposite of what I was saying. In other words, they walked away saying, "No way, that's wrong. I don't believe it. That's not for me. That's crazy; I could never think that way," etc., etc., and yet that, indeed, is what I have offered them. Or, they just enjoy my passion and don't think much about what I'm saying. Each person has their own unique way of interacting with other humans. I have come to a fun place of awareness on my path. I surf through the familiar outcomes with others and play with new things they share. I notice it gets better and better. Life is more fun every day. And it's not even a choice anymore. My energy is my energy. It shifts, changes, grows, retreats, becomes dirty, becomes clean, is powerful, is weak, and so on. Yet overall, in the constant flow of life, my energy becomes more and more happy as I watch myself enjoy my life and conquer my challenges. It's almost as if I started living my life over after my spiritual awakening. Suddenly someone said,

"Go, you're on!" and since then, everything that happened before it, and everything that's happened since, has had more meaning, and I am in awe.

I do not know many people who are able to move through life on this planet in a state of bliss, and those who do, I admire. I see so much struggle and daily negativity to deal with for many of us. We each have our sets of beliefs about love, sex, money, honesty, etiquette, business, leadership, politics, parenting, schooling, and community, among other things. Undoubtedly we see people colliding with others who do not share the same ideas, or we ourselves are colliding with others who do not share the same ideas. What I have learned in the last few years about circumstances, forgiveness, and the forgetting, is that moving forward from hard times and moving on, without blame, has helped me greatly in terms of inner peace. Things set us off. Someone does a certain thing that is offensive to you. It could be a stranger on the road or at the store. It could be someone we're working with. It could be a loved one seeming to purposely betray, disrespect, and even humiliate you. As Don Miguel Ruiz wrote in *The Four Agreements*, "Don't take anything personally. Nothing others do is because of you." What I have discovered is that forgiveness is easier to accomplish when we begin to examine the beliefs we have that we are measuring others against.

True forgiveness comes when we examine what we have, what we are, and especially, how the circumstances we may have trouble forgiving have actually helped us.

When we sit in angry feelings toward another and cannot forgive them, I do know that we are giving our life, our time, our ticket for what we're doing here, over to that other person. However, it is for no one else to say what is good for you. Each person makes choices as to what to take with them, what to leave behind. Baggage, as they call it, is carrying around the pain and suffering of what circumstances have brought into your life. What I have learned to see is that when something happens in a painful way, and yet that circumstance leads to a better place, how could you not forgive the circumstance, even be grateful for it? Only by holding on to the pain of the moment in which it happened can you stay in unforgiveness. I believe that recalling and living in those moments of pain, taking them forward into a fresh new moment, taints every new moment, which could be limitless positive potential otherwise. We hang onto our belief that what someone did was wrong, even if it was the best thing that ever happened to us. For example when some situation or person is toxic to you, and yet you can't seem to release them or it from your life, isn't it a blessing when something ends that? Even if someone pushes you away from them in a giant torrent of insults, rage, and blame, and therefore remove themselves from your life, isn't that a blessing, if that's what you were trying to accomplish? Why must we carry on with anger and unforgiveness against them for the things they said and felt toward us?

What is right and what is wrong? Doesn't each person have a different opinion on that? Yes there is a need for societal leadership on some level and certain agreed norms. I'm talking about individual feelings and general happiness in relating to it all. Is it wrong to do things differently than someone else regarding money or sex for example? Is it wrong to kill? Always? Or are there some instances where it's allowed? Who the hell is the authority who decides? Can we not all agree that many people think differently? If you are passionate about your point of view, that's great, but if you are dealing with someone who thinks differently, and all it does is make you angry, then you are saying you are right and they are wrong. Just because they don't agree with you. Do you realize how many people from your past could truly say that what *you* thought or did was wrong, even if it was not your intention? I enjoy a good debate, that ensues with respect. I am grateful to someone who can open my mind to more understanding. You can be right in your own mind, however it is an angry life to be angry with anyone that doesn't agree with you. Accept that some are indeed creating negativity and indeed creating suffering. However the energies of blame, revenge, vilify, punish, all stem from emotions that are toxic to the beholder, in my opinion. You will not understand why some do what they do, and they may not either. However we are all drops of water in the ocean of life, and you can just keep swimming towards more and more happiness and peace. Simply wish for what you want, and focus on it with unwavering faith. When things go awry, make your best choice and move forward. When you choose for you I believe it is for the highest and best of everyone around you too. Authenticity I believe is one of the most powerful positive energies we have to offer each other as humans.

All the parts of me that I became aware were limiting my happiness, and subsequently changed my behaviors and consciousness because of, still live within me. They were points of view, that did not serve my joy in life. They were my normal thinking at one point, and then as I desired to change them, they were something to watch come up and then let go of. They are still me. I lived that way before, there is a groove worn somewhere in my mind. I still can go there. However, they need not haunt me, or disturb me when they do come back. We are all the same, human. Each of us is capable of anything else one of us is capable of, and yet we are so different. Isn't it amazing how they say that each snowflake is unique, but

I see that together, on the ground, they turn into a united oneness, and quite a force. I no longer consider myself "over" anything, or changed for the better. Even when I say that! I simply strive to be happier, more accepting, and more satisfied. I am simply experiencing the life that I am in, knowing that it is extremely special and a gift, simply because no one else is living the same life I am. Not even those closest to me. We each see through our own past, present, and future, as a lens to the world. There are infinite possibilities in every moment. We just don't always see them. How could we, when the entire human race, planet Earth, and the unseen force that provides the energy making this movie called life all change, shift, and move constantly?

How is it that a human can have a heart that beats, providing power for its body for the length of a life? There is no charger, no plug, no cord. Where is that power coming from? These are the questions that I believe my higher self knows the answers to. In other words, there is a part of me, the unique human being called Jill, that somehow knows how amazing this whole game called life is. Who is running this game? I believe the goal of all that is, the beneficial energy that powers everything, is the same. It is an expansion. Building on each lifetime, the interactions of each energy with the other. For the fun of it, for the experience of it, for the unknown experiences, and shifts of creation that undoubtedly follow each new expansion of one's life, and love. It is what I've come to know as universal consciousness, a part of me, and of all, that knows what the greater pool of expansion and thought knows. How does one generation not know how to use computers, and the next does, seemingly from birth? This is the higher self that I am speaking of. There is a consciousness implanted into the human self that is born of the collective, but born into the personal identity. I have learned to enjoy my life more by trusting in my higher self.

There is GPS within us that is connected to the big picture. If we begin to trust that we do know best, that we are here for a reason—not a profession, but an expansion of human consciousness, which is pure enjoyment—we will begin to lighten up and believe that there is a constant stream of good behind us, pushing us to be all we can be for the simple purpose of enjoying our life and contributing to the enjoyment of others' lives. Each major human invention is preceded by collective desire and collective thought. Those whose thinking has expanded to ask for this brand new thing in this world have contributed to the bringing of it. The inventor is the first one to discover it, solve it, and bring it physically to others; the inventor has a gift of being an inventor. However, there is an underlying energy of his or her higher self, and the higher self of the collective, that is asking and assisting the inventor to bring this new creation into our material world, where it had not existed truly until that moment. At least not in the world as we know it. The history that we currently document on this planet is a very small amount of time, a blip on the radar, really, of the length of time that our planet points to having existed. Therefore, I believe it is quite egoic and small-minded to think that we know everything about what has come and gone before us and why.

My belief is that the human being is indeed our reality's greatest creation to date… but as such humanity comes with imperfect programming based on the evolutionary troubles it has faced so far. And yet, there is a perfect order to the universe, on its path of growth just like a tree. What part of the seed of a tree becomes the bark, and what part becomes the leaf? There is a perfect creative order working quietly in the unseen. A tree may not be able to communicate with us in our language, and may not feel pain or joy, but then again, we don't know for sure. All we know is that tree is part of our world, a wonderful part of our world, that is working alongside us in this life, and we are giving to each other. There is some kind of perfection in that.

When our loved ones die, we do not easily say good-bye. We are attached, and we miss them continuing alongside us in life. However, there is a greater essence to all things. The higher self. Somehow, somewhere, the universal intelligence is deciding what happens. But not in a small way that could fit inside our minds. That's why we cry "No!" We cry "Why? It does not feel right for me!" We say "I don't like it." And yet, the part of us that doesn't like it is probably just our little snowflake self that doesn't want to melt. That melted snowflake will transform back into snow again. Or will it? Perhaps it will become something else altogether. They say energy is neither created nor destroyed. Where this energy goes, I believe, is directed by our thoughts. As a human, with a powerful mind of intention that does influence outcomes, but also as a higher self. I believe that if we are generally unhappy, it is because we have not yet realized our divine nature, and that no matter what one person does, it happens for all of us. We are in this together, along with our Mother Earth, all of space we can see, and all of space that is beyond comprehension, and time for that matter. Our game called life is indeed a game. A game being played by a greater, higher force than our humanoid avatar player minds can comprehend, but can enjoy completely when we connect to the inner knowing that indeed it is all perfect.

Resources

Recommended Authors

Wayne Dyer

Louise Hay

Eckhart Tolle

Deepak Chopra

Jean Auel

Gary Douglas

Melody Beattie

Harriet Lerner

Abraham-Hicks Publications

Caroline Myss

Regena Thomashauer

Robert Scheinfeld

Iyanla Vanzant

Jack Canfield

Debbie Ford

Jill's Website

http://www.fairweathercenter.com/

About the Author

Jill Fairweather has always been involved in new endeavor after new endeavor, many at the same time. As a youngster, there was gymnastics, softball, unicycle, French horn and a paper route. Continually delving into her newest passion with enthusiasm, she worked in a number of industries before being recruited into real estate in 1997. In the real estate industry, she quickly ended up a workaholic. During a mid-life crisis she discovered her psychic gifts and her true spirituality. This amazing discovery has pulled her toward her true calling. Since then she has slowed down to smell the roses, something that those closest to her had always hoped she'd do! Her spiritual awakening has given her the power to accomplish even more, helping people more deeply than she ever had before.